Communication and Change

How to Motivate and Inspire Others

Table of Contents

Chapter 1. Introduction

Delve into a world where words can move mountains, and change becomes not a factor of fear, but a catalyst to phenomenal growth. Our Special Report titled "Communication and Change: How to Motivate and Inspire Others" identifies the key role communication plays in motivating change and inspiring others in any setting, from personal growth to corporate transformation. This easily digestible report illuminates the process, packed with real-world cases, expert insights, and innovative strategies to help you become a skilled communicator capable of sparking remarkable change. Let's embark on this exciting journey together and explore how persuasive communication can turn big ideas into reality. Don't miss this opportunity to learn, evolve, and shine. Your journey to becoming a catalyst for positive change starts right here, right now!

Chapter 2. Understanding the Power of Communication

In an era teeming with unprecedented change and challenges, harnessing communication's potent force has never been more critical. Communication is the fulcrum around which our lives revolve, fostering connections, promoting action, and inciting transformation. We begin by establishing a clear understanding of what communication is and its unignorable influence on our lives.

2.1. Demystifying Communication

Communication is like the oxygen we breathe, an invisible force vital to our survival and functioning as a society. The essence of communication is the successful transfer of information from one entity to another. However, this process isn't purely transactional; it is purpose-driven, rooted in the need to inspire a certain response or influence behavior.

Similarly, the complexity of communication cannot be understated. It is an amalgamation of verbal cues, non-verbal signals, and even silence, all carrying a wealth of meaning and relying on context for interpretation. Language, tone, gestures, facial expressions, and even the frequency and timing of communication, all contribute to the transmitted message and ultimately the receiver's derived interpretation and response.

2.2. Impact of Effective Communication

Effective communication bears the potential to shape societies, steer industries and transform individuals. It erases ambiguity, stirs understanding, engenders respect and fosters trust. Every negotiation, every agreement, every sapling of an idea that burgeons into a revolution has at its heart, the power of effective communication.

This dynamic ability of communication to inspire, motivate, and revolutionize makes it a key driver for transformative change. A leader's charismatic address can spur his team to peak performance. A compelling narrative shared across a company can cultivate a culture of innovation. A tactfully crafted advertisement can influence consumer behavior, spelling success for a product.

2.3. The Psychology Behind Communication

Effective communication draws heavily from our understanding of human psychology. Knowledge about how individuals perceive, process, and react to information can influence message crafting and delivering strategies. Understanding psychological aspects such as attention spans, cognitive biases, emotional triggers, the persuasion principles could play a pivotal role in enhancing communication effectiveness.

Emotion, for instance, strongly shapes how one interprets and responds to a message. A 2017 psychological study found that emotionally charged words significantly affected participants' ability to recall information. Similarly, researchers have long established the critical impact of storytelling in communication. Stories, packed with emotions, metaphors, and vivid visuals, can facilitate the processing and retention of complex information.

2.4. Communication as a Catalyst for Change

As an enabler of change, communication fuels the propagation of new ideas, solicits support, negates resistance, and facilitates the transition from the old to the new. Information, motivation, and positivity - the three critical prerequisites for change cascade through effective communication.

The 'Town Hall' meeting culture evolved in corporate settings serves as an apt example. These regular meetings, marked by an open exchange of thoughts between the company leadership and its employees, breed a culture of transparency and mutual respect. The platform facilitates sharing of company progress, upcoming changes, and also encourages employees to voice their concerns or suggestions.

2.5. Mastering the Art of Communication

Any endeavor to master communication must begin with active listening. Listening allows us to understand the perspectives and emotions of the speaker, to reciprocate effectively, and to adapt our message to the context and the audience. Furthermore, emotional intelligence and empathy are the hallmarks of an effective communicator. They equip us to resonate with the emotions of our audience and to deliver messages that connect and inspire.

Similarly, clarity and brevity in communication are paramount. As American statesman Henry Kissinger voiced, "The task of the leader is to get their people from where they are to where they have not been." To transport them over this abyss, the leader must paint a lucid picture of the intended outcome, the steps needed to achieve it, the challenges that might surface, and the strategies to overcome them.

Effective communicators also embrace feedback, using it constructively to adjust and improve their communication. They appreciate the diverse backgrounds, perspectives, and receptive capacities of their audience, and tailor their messages accordingly. They refrain from using jargon and overly intricate language that could lead to misinterpretation.

In conclusion, understanding the power of communication is not a mere theoretical exercise. It is a venture towards unlocking the colossal potential it bears, inventing ceaselessly new ways to infuse passion, incite action, inspire change, and sculpt progress. This journey, however exciting and rewarding, is one of continuous learning and practice. As American political scientist Harold Lasswell famously pitched, communication is all about 'Who says what, to whom, why, to what effect?'

Chapter 3. Decoding the Elements of Persuasive Communication

Persuasion is a craft honed over time, and the very foundation of this art is communication. The right approach to communication has the power to move minds, inspire actions, and foster positive changes, within individuals and larger communities alike. To fully grasp the concept of persuasive communication, it's imperative to understand its components and how to weave them in our day-to-day interactions.

3.1. Understanding the Concept of Persuasion in Communication

The first step towards mastering persuasive communication is decoding the concept of persuasion. It is the process of influencing someone's belief, attitude, intentions, motivations, or behaviors. In an organizational perspective, the ability to persuade others is a vital skill that leaders, innovators, and changemakers should possess.

Persuasion in communication is not about manipulation; rather, it supports an open exchange of ideas and encourages dialogue. This shows that the intent is not to control but to co-create a solution or change beneficial to all parties involved. Hence, understanding the expectations, perceptions and concerns of the individuals you're communicating with is crucial.

3.2. The Intersection of Empathy and Persuasion

A pivotal element in mastering the art of persuasion is the ability to empathize with others. Understanding and acknowledging the perspectives, emotions and experiences of your counterparts paves the way for more open, honest, and successful communications.

By displaying genuine empathy in your communication style, you encourage a space of trust and openness—necessary prerequisites for effective persuasion. Empathy allows you to tap into the needs of others, enabling you to tailor your persuasion techniques accordingly. This concept is expertly summarized in the timeless quote, "People don't care how much you know until they know how much you care."

3.3. Theoretical Foundations: Ethos, Pathos, and Logos

The art of persuasion, as conceptualized by Aristotle, comprises three fundamental components: ethos, pathos, and logos.

Ethos involves establishing your credibility or character in the eyes of your listeners. It signifies that you are trustworthy, knowledgeable, and possess the necessary expertise.

Pathos touches upon the emotional aspect of persuasion. It involves understanding the audience's beliefs, values, and feelings and using this knowledge to create a passionate, emotional connection.

Logos, on the other hand, focuses on logical and factual evidence. This technique involves providing a well-rounded argument supported by facts, statistics, and figures. Proper use of logos adds weight to your message and helps others see reason in your proposition.

3.4. Crafting a Statement of Purpose

Every persuasive communication should unfold from a clear and compelling statement of purpose. This encapsulates the reason for the communication – the change you wish to bring about and why. This statement should be concise, sincere, and powerful enough to pique the audience's interest and earn their initial agreement.

Represent your ideas in a format that aligns with your audience's concerns or values. Evoking shared interests or common goals can stimulate an emotional response and increase the persuasiveness of your communication.

3.5. Storytelling: The Key to Capturing Interest

People have been telling stories since time immemorial to transfer wisdom, values, and lessons. Stories help to humanize messages and make your communication relatable.

When it comes to persuasion, storytelling serves to activate the listeners' brains, making them more receptive and empathetic. It allows you to demonstrate your values and point of view in a non-threatening way, capturing your audience's interest and facilitating easier understanding of your perspectives.

3.6. Constructive Arguments and Counterarguments

Transparent and open dialogue is the backbone of persuasive communication. Openly discussing not just your arguments but potential counterarguments strengthens your proposition. Anticipating what your listeners might say in response allows you to be prepared with well-thought-out responses that acknowledge their concerns and yet make a strong case for your ideas.

Constructing an argument with thoughtful counterarguments reduces resistance, increases credibility, and shows regard for others' opinions, driving the persuasive process forward.

3.7. Assertive Yet Respectful Communication

An essential component of persuasive communication is assertiveness. This denotes the ability to get your point across without being rude or disrespectful. A persuasive communicator knows how to assert their position and needs while also considering the positions and needs of others.

Balancing assertiveness and respectfulness is pivotal. One must delicately navigate this equilibrium to ensure your ideas are taken seriously, without belittling or intimidating others.

3.8. Mastering Non-Verbal Cues

Often, it's not what you say but how you say it. Non-verbal cues such as body language, eye contact, facial expression, and posture play a significant role in persuasion. Positive body language can help create a better rapport with the audience, making them more receptive to your message, thereby enhancing your persuasive power.

Remember, mastering the elements of persuasive communication is not an ultramarathon but a journey. With consistent practice and refinement of the techniques highlighted above, you'll find yourself capable of manifesting change and inspiring others through the magic of your words. This foundation equips you to effectively use communication as a tool for change, making you a catalyst for positive growth. Explore this journey of change and nourish the seeds of your learning with the wealth of knowledge and growth that only persuasive communication can bring.

Chapter 4. Navigate Through Change: Why It Matters?

At the intersection of our present and future lies the inevitability of change. A myriad of factors necessitates the existence of change, the principle being evolution. As humans, we are designed to grow, learn, adapt, and handle new circumstances. Our inherent resistance to such alterations, however, often impairs the process of change. In understanding why we should navigate through change, we must illuminate its significance and democratize the process.

4.1. The Protagonist of Growth

Change, fundamentally, marks progress. Imperceptible or palpable, voluntary or involuntary, it is the silent driver of maturation – personal, professional, or societal. It propels us out from stagnation, invites innovation, and enriches perspectives.

Imagine a world unaltered by change; static, monotonous, devoid of exploration and expansion. It is an unsettling thought to reside in an era devoid of progression, a testament to our inherent reliance on change. Grasping the undercurrent of this reality, we invite upon ourselves an opportunity to consciously navigate through it.

4.2. The Inevitability of Change

As sure as the rotation of the earth around the sun, change is inevitable. The world is dynamically evolving, with profound alterations shaping human life and the environment alike. From technological advancements to shifts in socio-economic scenarios, the domain of change expands vastly with time.

Understanding that change is a constant phenomenon, it becomes a practical necessity to navigate through this labyrinth. With this awareness, we prepare ourselves to face unexpected circumstances, adapt to new modes of life, and participate proactively in shaping our destinies.

4.3. The Psychological Aspect

Tackling resistance is a crucial part in the navigation through change. Often rooted in fear, habit, or uncertainty, resistance is inherently human but counterproductive in the journey of growth. By confronting these deterrents, we gradually attune ourselves to welcome change.

Understanding that fear of the unknown often fuels resistance provides us with tools to combat it. Taking calculated risks, seeking counseling, or engaging in inspiring, forward-thinking discussions can help dismantle the formidable walls of fear. Slowly but steadily, the path to navigating change transforms from a dread-laden journey to a cycle of growth and opportunities.

4.4. Learning Through Change

Our experiences during periods of change serve as veritable life lessons. Change equips us with survival skills, problem-solving abilities, resilience, and much more. As we traverse these times of alteration, we inadvertently learn, adapt, and grow.

Recognizing that each instance of change is a podium of learning, we discover a new roadmap for navigating future alterations. These are crucial life skills that fortify us against adversity and cultivate a growth mindset, enabling us to face the subsequent stages of change with an invigorated spirit.

4.5. Becoming Agents of Change

Understanding the significance of navigating through change bestows upon us a powerful realization – we can be agents of change. Armed with the knowledge and skills to facilitate change, we can influence others, shaping societal structures, workplaces, and personal lives. Thus, the personal journey of navigating change converges onto a larger, collective path.

By spearheading adaptations and displaying resilience, we inspire others to embrace and navigate changes. This role not only enhances our own lives but also creates a ripple effect of transformative potentials, propelling humanity further down the path of evolution and growth.

In summation, change is a multifaceted phenomenon. Navigating through change enables us to grow personally and professionally, promotes resilience, inculcates life skills, and potentially influences others. Recognizing this significance marks the first step towards a constructive relationship with change. From here, the journey towards becoming skilled navigators of change begins. The immense scope of this exploration has the power to motivate, enlighten, and kindle uncharted realms of possibilities within us. Change, it appears, is the catalyst we never knew we needed.

This transformational journey would be incomplete without delving deeper into the fascinating associations between communication and change. Anticipate exploring this confluence in the following chapters, where we uncover the persuasive power of communication and its cardinal role in advocating change. From theory to practice, this excursion promises to be intriguing and enlightening, heralding a vibrant exploration of the hidden potential within us.

Chapter 5. The Role of Communication in Inspiring Change

At a fundamental level, communication is the exchange of information between individuals. It's critical to all aspects of life, influencing our relationships, our work, and our understanding of the world. When it comes to inspiring change, communication assumes a catalyst role. This chapter will delve into the importance of communication in evoking transformation, touching upon various strategies, real-life instances, and expert perspectives.

5.1. The Power of Communication

Consider the leaders that have brought significant changes in society - Martin Luther King Jr., Mahatma Gandhi, or Nelson Mandela. They, among other things, were phenomenal communicators. Their words moved people, provoked thought, and rallied them towards a shared cause.

Communication wields power; it possesses the potential to inspire change. The key lies in employing it effectively, with transparency, empathy, and clarity. This isn't solely about using large words or grand phrases; it's about making messages relatable, inspiring, and actionable.

5.2. The Critical Need for Communication in Change

Change, by its very nature, is intrinsically unsettling. This holds true in both personal and organizational contexts. We're creatures of habit, and change takes us out of our comfort zone. It's where the role of communication becomes vital.

Transparent communication channels during periods of change can help mitigate fears and uncertainties. Adequately communicated change helps create realistic expectations, reducing the odds of disappointment or shock down the line. It not only provides a sense of purpose but also ensures all stakeholders are on the same page and working towards a shared goal. Efficacy in communication can mean the difference between smooth transitions and disruptive chaos.

5.3. Communication Strategies for Inspiring Change

When directing communication towards inspiring change, it becomes crucial to implement certain strategies.

1. Transparency: Honesty is imperative when managing change. Transparent communication fosters trust and allows for genuine conversations about why change is necessary and how it will benefit individuals and the organization as a whole.

2. Empathy: Empathetic communication allows leaders to connect with the emotions of their team, understand their fears, and tailor their communication to address these effectively. This approach can facilitate smoother implmentation of change.

3. Timely Communication: Prompt and regular communication is essential during periods of change. It reduces uncertainty and alleviates concerns.

4. Clear Messaging: Vague communication often results in misunderstandings and resistance. Therefore, it's crucial to provide clear, concise information that leaves no room for confusion.

5. Two-Way Communication: Communication should be interactive. This encourages feedback and engages everyone in the change process, making them feel heard and valued.

5.4. Case Study: Microsoft's Cultural Shift

The transformation of Microsoft under CEO Satya Nadella, marked by a shift from a 'know-it-all' to 'learn-it-all' mindset, presents a prominent example of communication inspiring change.

Nadella's transparent communication about the changes he intended to make, along with his empathy towards employees' fears, laid a solid foundation for Microsoft's transformation. His clear messaging not only instilled a sense of purpose throughout the organization but also helped align all stakeholders towards a common vision.

The leadership's consistent and two-way communication ensured the entire organization remained interconnected and informed. This helped alleviate concerns, and the continuous engagement encouraged employees to link their individual growth with the organization's transformation, thereby enhancing the change process.

5.5. Conclusion

In conclusion, communication is an essential driving force behind inspiring change. The way a message is delivered can influence how change is perceived and accepted. Harnessing the power of effective communication can turn any individual into an agent of extraordinary change, capable of moving mountains with words alone.

The journey to becoming a better communicator and thus a catalyst of change is a rewarding one, steeped in self-improvement, personal growth, and the potential to positively impact countless lives. With the right strategies, mindset, and persistent practice, you can wield the power of communication to instigate invaluable transformations in your life and the world around you.

Chapter 6. Building Bridges: Inspiring and Leading Through Communication

Communication, a multifaceted mechanism that synchronizes human cognition to achieve shared goals, is the bedrock of leadership. Inspirational leaders have always harnessed the power of language to spark a desire for change, foster resilience, and engage diverse people towards realizing a shared vision.

The process of communicating change can be likened to building bridges - forging links between the status quo and the envisioned future, between individuals, and between different ideas, emotions, and realities. This chapter will delve into how leaders can utilize effective communication to inspire, motivate, and lead their teams or communities.

6.1. Leveraging the Power of Emotional Intelligence in Communication

Emotional Intelligence (EI), the capability to recognize, comprehend, utilize, and regulate emotions effectively, presents a profound tool for inspiring and guiding others. Leaders who encapsulate high levels of EI are likely to demonstrate superior capabilities to understand and manage their emotions and those of others.

Table 1. Leveraging Emotional Intelligence in Communication

Understand Yourself	Understand Others	Act Responsibly
Recognize your own emotions and their impact on your behavior	Show empathy by recognizing and understanding others' emotions	Regulate your emotions and react appropriately to the emotions of others
Develop self-awareness and identify your strengths and weaknesses	Respect other's perspectives and responses	Consider the emotional context when making decisions
Learn to adapt your communication style based on your emotions and the situation	Develop open communication lines that encourage emotional expression	Implement actions that encourage positive emotional expression in your team or community

6.2. Building Trust Through Authentic Communication

Building trust is a critical component of effective leadership and communication plays a crucial role in this process. A leader's ability to communicate authentically and transparently can effectively create a climate of trust.

Authentic Communication Practices

- Honesty Above All: Always be honest, even when the truth is uncomfortable. Authentic leaders do not distort the truth to meet their ends.

- Consistency Counts: Consistency in your words and actions establishes your credibility as a leader.

- Understand and Meet Their Needs: Listen to understand people's needs and respond to them effectively. Your credibility increases when you respond to those needs authentically.

- Show Empathy: Understanding and sharing others' feelings and problems demonstrates that you value them as individuals.

- Admit Mistakes: Authentic leaders are not afraid to admit their mistakes. They accept their faults and learn from them, which others respect.

6.3. Encouraging Change Through Narrative Leadership

Narrative leadership is a novel and potent tool that uses storytelling as a medium to encourage change. Often, numbers, data, and bullet points are not enough to persuade people to change. A compelling narrative, however, can stir emotions and encourage change on a deeper level.

Narrative Leadership Strategies

- Personalize Your Message: Sharing personal stories can bring your vision to life and create an emotional connection to the change you propose.

- Show Don't Tell: A powerful story must show the implications of change rather than telling them.

- Simplicity is Key: Keep your story simple and clear. Overcomplication can lead to confusion or misinterpretation.

- Add a Human Element: Stories should include human elements to which the listeners can relate.

- Be Sincere: Sincerity is vital for authenticity. If you don't believe in your story, no one else will.

6.4. Instilling a Growth Mindset Through Communication

A growth mindset fosters an understanding that abilities can be developed through dedication and hard work. This perspective creates a passion for learning and a resilience essential for great accomplishment.

Communicating with a growth mindset requires acknowledging and valuing effort, process, and progress. Leaders should deliver feedback constructively, focusing on the process rather than the person, demonstrating belief in their ability to grow, and offering strategies for development.

6.5. Conclusion

The journey from being a communicator to becoming an inspirational leader is as intricate as building bridges - a process of understanding, connecting, and leading. Embracing emotional intelligence, fostering trust, leveraging the power of storytelling, and promoting a growth mindset can catapult your communication prowess, transforming you into an inspirational figure capable of instigating meaningful change. Communication is the lifeblood of leadership and change - master it and watch mountains move. Remember, change is not something to be feared; instead, embrace it, for change is growth.

Chapter 7. Strategies to Motivate Others Using Effective Communication

Effective communication has always been at the core of successful leadership. Herein, we'll try to explore multiple strategies to motivate and inspire others using this vital tool.

7.1. Understanding Your Audience

The first step in any communication process is understanding your audience. Effective communication is a two-way process that involves understanding the individual needs, backgrounds, and perspectives of your audience. Learn about their values, beliefs, fears, and challenges. This will allow you to tailor your message in a way that is most likely to resonate with them and inspire action.

In order to truly understand your audience, invest time in interacting with them. Conduct surveys, polls, or one-on-one interviews to gain deeper insights about their aspirations and concerns.

7.2. The Power of Listening

Listening is just as crucial, if not more so, than speaking when it comes to effective communication. Active listening is when you attentively listen and respond to the speaker in a way that improves mutual understanding. This can be done by paraphrasing what they say, asking clarifying questions, or merely nodding to show you are engaged.

Listening allows you to gauge the mindset, motives, and feelings of the speaker, which helps in constructing a message that triggers action. It also makes them feel valued, openly leading to increased trust and rapport.

7.3. Framing the Message

Framing is an essential skill in communication. It involves presenting the information in a way that the audience perceives it in your intended way and motivates them to action. Maintain a positive and optimistic tone, even when dealing with challenges or discussing changes.

When framing your message, always focus on the benefits, painting a clear picture of what success looks like. Instead of saying, "We need to work extra hours to finish this project," you could frame it positively by saying, "By putting in some additional hours, we'll successfully deliver this project which could open up opportunities for promotions and incentives."

7.4. Transparency and Authenticity

Be transparent when communicating with your team. Share the 'why' behind every major decision. When people understand the reasons behind various actions, they are more likely to commit to the change.

Authenticity is also key. Share personal experiences and show vulnerability. This makes you relatable and trust-worthy, thereby enhancing the acceptability of the message you are delivering.

7.5. Inspiring Through Storytelling

Storytelling is a powerful communication tool that can inspire and motivate. Stories can stir emotions and spark the imagination, making the audience more receptive to the message.

Use personal stories or anecdotes to convey ideas or values

effectively. Stories could be about successful projects or initiatives, challenges overcome, or personal growth journeys.

Remember that stories should be relevant, engaging, and easy to understand. They should ideally evoke a strong emotional response from your audience and leave them with a memorable message.

7.6. Regular Feedback and Appreciation

Lastly, provide regular feedback and express appreciation for a job well done. Constructive feedback helps individuals grow, while regular appreciation recognizes their efforts, keeping them motivated.

When delivering feedback, use the 'sandwich method', which involves starting with an appreciation, followed by constructive criticism, and ending with positive reinforcement. This approach boosts the receiver's morale and receptiveness to feedback.

In conclusion, effective communication is an art that requires practice, patience, and dedication. But once mastered, it can be a powerful tool to motivate others and ensure successful leadership. Remember, people are more likely to follow leaders who communicate effectively, exhibit authenticity, and inspire by their actions and words. Always strive to be such a leader, and watch how your ability to motivate others transforms dramatically.

Chapter 8. Practical Case Studies: Communication Leading to Change

Communication isn't merely the act of exchanging words; rather, it is the art of transforming ideas into change, inspiring creativity, and enabling growth. Let's unravel this art through a series of practical case studies, dissecting how effective communication leads to unprecedented changes.

8.1. Case Study 1: Fiat Chrysler's Organizational Change

Renowned organization Fiat Chrysler moved mountains when it flipped the traditional corporate model upside down. They recognized that effective internal communication amongst employees was paramount in facilitating change.

The CEO at the time, Sergio Marchionne, initiated a radical restructure. His priority was to reduce the hierarchy, enhancing communication streams throughout the company. Information flowed freely from top to bottom and vice versa without the typical bureaucratic hindrances.

Utilizing regular town hall meetings and digital discussions forums, they created a culture of openness and transparency. This built trust and encouraged employees to adopt the new strategy, thereby creating an atmosphere for positive change.

Marchionne's consistent and clear communication left no room for ambiguity. Employees knew the purpose and goals of the change, which prevent confusion or resistance. His leadership style was characterized by communication open and honest communication.

8.2. Case Study 2: The Transformation of LEGO

LEGO, the toy-production giant, faced a nearly catastrophic financial crisis in the early 2000s. The solution was a top-to-bottom restructuring, and pivotal to this transformation was clear, inspiring communication.

LEGO decided to reduce its product line by approximately 60%, a major change that required buy-in from every member of the organization. To achieve this, management employed effective communication strategies – ensuring everyone understood the necessity of the change and felt part of it.

The company also optimized communication with their customer base. They started to listen more to the consumers and took their input seriously. This informed change in their production led to products that customers genuinely wanted, fostering record-breaking sales and company growth.

8.3. Case Study 3: Microsoft's Shift to Cloud-Based Services

Microsoft made a massive shift from traditional software to cloud-based services like Office 365 and Azure. Such a significant change required a reimagining of the entire company's architecture and an overhaul of their underlying methods of operation.

CEO Satya Nadella spearheaded the revolution, employing communication as his primary tool. Every strategy and process change was communicated in a clear and concise manner, ensuring that all employees were on the same page.

Intra-company communication was encouraged via collaborative platforms like Yammer, with a strong emphasis on sharing ideas and feedback. This helped to foster a culture of unity as everyone worked towards the shared goal.

Nadella also fostered communication with stakeholders and customers, reassuring them about the changes, and helping them to understand the benefits of the new services. This external communication was critical in gaining acceptance and adoption of the shifting model.

8.4. Case Study 4: IBM's Reinvention

IBM underwent multiple transformations in its corporate history. It pivoted from a hardware company to a software-oriented one, and then again to its present focus on cloud-based services and cognitive computing.

Throughout their transitions, IBM relied heavily on communication. They built an internal social network, allowing communication streams between different teams and enhancing collaboration. IBM also promoted transparency through company-wide quarterly progress updates.

Externally, IBM directed its communication towards educating customers about the potential benefits of their new services. By delivering a clear and compelling message, they turned potential resistance into acceptance and, eventually, enthusiasm for their innovative solutions.

These case studies demonstrate the power of effective communication, highlighting its significance in driving successful change. In the forthcoming section, we will dive deeper into communication strategies and techniques that pave the way for effective change management. Take away lessons from these transformations, and apply them in your respective spheres, whether you are a CEO orchestrating a corporate restructuring, or an individual hoping to inspire change in your community.

The power to inspire and motivate change truly lies in our words and how we choose to communicate them.

Chapter 9. Dealing with Resistance: Transforming Negativity into Positivity

No change ever unfolds without resistance—a natural, human reaction spurred by apprehension or fear of the unknown. But when channeled right, this resistance can be transformed into an impetus for positivity and personal growth. This chapter takes a deep dive into the art of dealing with resistance, turning the walls of negativity into bridges of positivity.

9.1. The Nature of Resistance

Human nature often dictates a preference for the familiar, the known—creating a natural tendency to resist change. Change brings with it a level of uncertainty, a shifting of comfort zones and a disruption to our normal routines. It threatens the status quo, making us question our perceptions, beliefs, and actions, thereby sparking resistance.

Resistance can be both overt and covert. While overt resistance includes clear refusal or opposition to change, covert resistance is more subtle—it could be procrastination or delay, undermining a change initiative, or a lack of participation. Each form must be identified and addressed distinctly for successful change management.

9.2. Identifying Resistance

Recognizing resistance in its early stages paves the way for a smoother change trajectory. Indicators could be a decrease in productivity, a surge in errors, an increase in staff turnover, or disengaged employees. These signals should be diligently attended to solve the issues at the root.

Understanding the reasons behind resistance is crucial. This could be due to the fear of unknown outcomes, loss of job security, increased workload, or failure to see the benefits of the change. Addressing these reasons makes it easier to rally support for change.

9.3. The Power of Communication

Communication serves as a bridge between uncertainty and understanding. Encouraging open communication can minimize resistance by gently addressing fears and fostering a supportive environment.

Efficient communication occurs on two levels - information sharing and active listening. While providing employees with an understanding of why the change is necessary, it is equally important to hear their concerns. Let them voice their fears—this shows empathy and support, reducing resistance and creating an environment conducive to change.

9.4. Handling Resistance: Strategies

Several strategies can be applied to tackle resistance efficiently.

1. Direct Involvement: Encourage those resisting to involve in the change process actively. This not only informs them about why the change is necessary but also provides them with a sense of control over the change.

2. Training and Counseling: Arrange workshops, training, or counseling sessions to help employees acclimate to the change. This can build confidence and help them transition smoothly.

3. Negotiation and Agreement: Sometimes, negotiation can provide

a way forward. Offering incentives to those strongly opposed to change can help secure their cooperation.

4. Top-Down Support: Garner the support of leaders within the organization. A clear message from leadership in favor of the change can reduce resistance.

5. Positive Reinforcement: Applaud those who embrace change. Positive reinforcement can motivate others to follow suit.

9.5. From Negativity to Positivity

Transforming resistance into positivity is no easy feat. It involves understanding human emotions, developing solid communication strategies, and integrating these strategies seamlessly into the change process.

Celebrate small victories, recognize and reward resilience in face of change, and lead by example. Use resistance as a teaching moment to showcase how change can bring about personal and professional growth.

Stress on the benefits of change—enhanced skills, opportunities for advancement, personal growth, and accomplishment. This shift in perspective can create a positive environment, turning opposition into opportunity.

In conclusion, resistance to change is inherent. But with the right approach, this resistance can be molded into positivity that acts as a catalyst for change. The key lies in understanding, empathizing, communicating, and integrating these strategies into your journey through change. Through patience and perseverance, transformation can be less a mountain to conquer and more an adventure to undertake, one step at a time.

Chapter 10. Inspiring the Next Generation: Communication and Leadership

In the grand theater of life, inspiring the next generation is not a luxury but a necessity. This responsibility typically rests on the shoulders of leaders who have the power of communication at their disposal to show the way forward, to motivate and to inspire. Powerful, persuasive communication thus becomes an indispensable tool for leaders of the future as they step up to the task of guiding the next generation.

10.1. The Power of Persuasive Communication

Persuasive communication is an art well understood by today's most successful leaders. It involves not only being able to effectively articulate an idea or argument but also to resonate with the listener at an emotional level. As long-term sustainability becomes the critical watchword for all successful organizations, leaders who can effectively communicate the importance and values of sustainable practices are increasingly prized.

How do you cultivate persuasive communication skills? It starts with consistency. Your messages must provide a consistent framework, demonstrating stability and reliability. Secondly, sincerity is crucial. People, particularly the next generation, can sense authenticity. If you engage in communication simply to manipulate or gain something, your audience will notice. You need to be genuinely invested in the topic at hand to effectively persuade others of its

importance. Show your passion and it will become infectious —
provoking interest and triggering meaningful conversations.

10.2. Influencing through Empathetic Leadership

Empathy is a powerful trait in leadership. It allows leaders to
understand and share the feelings of others, making them more
approachable and relatable. Empathy fosters an atmosphere of trust,
respect, and understanding, building stronger, more productive
relationships.

Yet, empathy must extend beyond face-to-face interactions.
Communication, specifically written and spoken word, is a vital
medium through which leaders can express empathy. By
understanding the perspectives and feelings of others, you create
messages that resonate strongly with your audience. Acknowledging
their experiences, showing sensitivity to their needs, and expressing
genuine concern for their well-being, can deeply impact how your
message is received. Only such an empathetic approach to
communication can truly inspire and create buy-in from the next
generation.

10.3. Storytelling: Bringing Ideas to Life

Arguably, one of the most effective ways to inspire and engage others
is through storytelling. Stories can make complex ideas more
digestible, bring people together, inspire action, and spark emotions.
Importantly, great stories often stay with us, helping to create a
lasting connection with the storyteller and the message being
conveyed.

Leaders can leverage the power of storytelling to communicate their vision, share lessons learned, or to paint a picture of future success. It's all about making the message compelling and relatable; well-told narratives often trump the most scientific data or statistical evidence.

Organizational leaders can share stories about the company's journey, its achievements, and the hurdles overcome along the way. Or they could narrate tales of individuals whose cooperation and zeal helped the company surpass its goals. Stories like these foster unity, strengthen organizational culture, and inspire employees to strive for success.

10.4. Encouraging Open Dialogue and Feedback

Inspiring the next generation isn't a one-way street. It's not just about delivering impactful speeches, telling compelling stories, or demonstrating strong and empathetic leadership qualities. It's equally about encouraging the brewing of fresh ideas, contributing to thoughtful dialogue, and cultivating a culture of continuous feedback.

Inclusion in communication is vital. Effective leaders understand this and tirelessly work towards involving their teams in decision-making processes and policy alterations. When the next generation feels their voices are being heard, they are more likely to commit to the leader's vision, showing enhanced productivity and contributing to robust, sustainable growth.

10.5. Conclusion

Inspiring the next generation requires effective communication and strong leadership skills. Leaders must persuade confidently, showing sincerity and consistency in their messaging. They must display empathy, understanding the feelings and perspectives of those they lead. Using storytelling can bring ideas to life, creating a lasting connection with those you're attempting to inspire. Lastly, promoting an open dialogue and feedback culture can make your team feel included and valued, building loyalty and commitment.

As we step into a future where these skills become more critical, leaders should focus on becoming more effective communicators. After all, inspiring the next generation will directly impact our societies, economies, and the world as a whole. It is a pivotal role that falls to our leaders who possess the power to shape the future through their words and actions.

Chapter 11. Future Trends: The Evolving Dynamics of Communication and Change

The evolution of communication in the last few decades has radically changed how we convey and absorb information, transforming our societies and workplaces. As change accelerates, the dynamics between communication and change also continue to evolve, propelled by technological advancements, societal shifts, and generational transitions.

11.1. A Look into the Cyber Space: Technology and Communication

With the growing importance of digital technology, internet-based communication tools have broken down geographic barriers, allowing instantaneous connection with people worldwide. Email, video conferencing, social media, and other innovations provide rapid, cost-effective methods of communication, revolutionizing business strategies, customer engagement, and human interaction.

This shift to digital communication has widened the reach for information dissemination, which plays a critical role during times of change. With a simple click, changes can be communicated across organizations and societies. However, the digital frontier also presents challenges. The risk of miscommunication increases with the absence of physical cues in digital communication. Additionally, the rapid proliferation of information can lead to misinformation if not properly managed. Therefore, ensuring clear and accurate digital communication is crucial in change management.

11.2. Generational Shift: The New Office Speak

As older generations retire, younger generations who are digital natives are beginning to dominate workplaces. Millennials and Generation Z carry a unique set of values, preferences, and communication styles that heavily influence the evolving dynamics of communication during change.

Social consciousness, personal growth, and inclusivity are key for these generations. They appreciate transparent, open dialogue and participative decision-making processes. Therefore, top-down, one-way communication rarely resonates with them; instead, they might welcome change more readily if they are involved in the process. As this demographic shift continues, future trends in communication during change will likely involve more bottom-up, reciprocal, and democratic communication strategies.

11.3. The Power of Storytelling

While data and facts provide the backbone for any change initiative, human beings inherently gravitate towards stories. Hence, the emerging trend of storytelling in communication, particularly in change initiatives. Effective storytelling can build a bridge between the abstract nature of change and the tangible realities faced by people. A well-crafted narrative can motivate and inspire people, create a shared understanding, and humanize the process of change.

Rather than presenting change as a list of impersonal data points, painting a vivid picture of the change's purpose, the journey ahead, and the desirable future state can foster emotional connection and buy-in. This trend is poised to gain more traction, making storytelling an essential tool in the communicator's playbook.

11.4. Emotional Intelligence and Empathy: The Soft Side of Communication

With increasing recognition of the importance of soft skills, emotional intelligence, and empathy are emerging as vital dimensions of communication during change. Changes, especially those that are sudden or major, can fuel a multitude of emotions ranging from anxiety to excitement. Leaders who can demonstrate emotional intelligence by recognizing and validating these feelings can open channels for more authentic dialogue. Furthermore, displaying empathy can build trust, reassure individuals, and ultimately ease the transition process. Therefore, imbuing communication with emotional intelligence and empathy is likely to become a more prominent trend.

11.5. Blurring Boundaries: The Interplay of Personal and Professional Lives

With the futuristic concept of 'work-life integration' gradually replacing 'work-life balance', the separation between personal and professional lives is blurring. As a result, the future could witness a trend towards a more comprehensive approach to communication during change. Rather than only focusing on the professional impact of change, acknowledging its personal implications might become more pertinent.

In summary, the future trends of communication during change are likely to be shaped by growing digitalization, demographic shifts, the power of storytelling, emotional intelligence, and a more comprehensive understanding of the change impact. By keeping abreast of these trends and flexibly adapting to them, anyone can become a skilled communicator, adeptly navigating change and inspiring a shared vision within their personal or professional sphere.

The confluence of communication and change is rich with potential for transformation, and as these dynamics continue to evolve, they offer us new ways to motivate, inspire, and make a difference in our ever-changing world.